Prickly Kindness

Heather Finton

published 2017 by Northern Undercurrents

ISBN 978-0-9958247-2-0

cover artwork by Justien Senoa Wood

Thank you to my teachers' teachers,

who speak an array of languages

and help me find words in my own.

May we all keep paying attention.

Snap

Let me learn
how to love

fall consumed
by shine
on a leaf

hear the snap crackle pop
in your voice
even as I savour
my oatmeal

be licked
by stray dogs,
bring them home
without leashes

a pied piper
with a crippled heart
and dancing refugees

honouring sweet goodness
in all its forms.

Mid-life can be like
waking groggy
from an afternoon nap
with some regret
for the angle of the sun,
how the golden evening
is here
and there is still time
to play
but the day
is receding quickly.

Some go reeling
when they hear
the herald call
of dark,
frantic to stave off
inevitable shadows.

Some feel the late sunshine
pierce their hearts
and remake their agendas.

Me, I am so grateful
for my regrets,
how they teach me
depth of caring,
how the evening sun
puts haloes
on all that is here.

Help me to be horny
for joy
spreading through this wave
of muscles and sensations

not just my own
but all of us

feeding our appetites
for kindness

cleaning the air
with our choices

stopping the bombfall
because there are better games,
more heartfelt
ways to laugh

sharing food
because people we love
are hungry.

My best poems
are wordless

these glances exchanged,
a universe winking
to provoke my grin

the slight tilt of head
or hips

riding convergence

in ways that laugh
at language

cherishing
the sweet attempts

abandoned
fruitful
dandelion fluff,
pregnant in air.

A new way of losing
sounds depressing

but has the possibility
of graceful unwrapping

letting fall
protective shawls

giving away
what seemed precious

to let loss
become a gift

exploring dancing
with no legs

flattened on the floor

held in place
by tender gravity,

a force beyond understanding
cradling our exhaustion.

The forest was quiet
until I slowed to hear a tree

leaning on another;
a most particular creaking,
music of two
in forced proximity

one had been falling
but was caught

the standing tree
unhindered
in its view of sky

sounding a dissonant symphony
quite without intent,
two violinists
with bows entangled

their irregular melody
the strongest tune
until the rushing wind
blew like a harpist
over treetops

pointing to
unseen orchestra.

One morning
in a sunny room

there was a wail
and a fishing line
terribly tangled

not just one knot
but a mass of them
inexplicably complex.

Despite another plan,
that day had space
for kind attention,
for six hands
fighting despair
with curiosity

for courage to not run.

And though the plan
had pulled for a different happiness

time reeled us in
a hiss of nylon line
audible joy.

Stop
trying to be pretty
or organized

sink into your birthright

savoury soup,

a radical love

without borders,

an ornery gladness

full-throated,
feathers ruffling.

You know
what you need to

so stop

and go.

I don't care about poetry.

What I do
is take a lamb's corpse
and mourn
that it died too young

and gently skin what is there
and let the force of water
wash it clean

and light a fire of sage
to help with tanning

and pound and pound again

until the hide
is as supple
and translucent
as I can bear

and then I stumble with reverence
on one of the billion names for god
and wrap my offering around it.

I have been plucked
by invisible fingers

on strings I did not know were there
but vibrate deep
in the cave of pleasure
and open into sky

music like harp
or erotic guitar
or some other wire
with tones of brass and crystal

the hiss of steam
where water and fire
ignite
without drowning

the warm fog of being

flushing my face
naked in the world

no pretence of normal

twanging.

A grand laughter,

these masters,

men and women freed from need,
poking at greed

with their grins

and their tears rolling over upturned lips

...crazy fools indeed,

and the cries of their playtime

incite my dancing.

Caterpillar crawl
unbelievably tactile;
we say one hundred feet
but really they are more like fingers
or nipples
sensitive to branch and ground
constant seeking
testing the path
fluid sensory information
building direction,
provoking impetus.

Surely such a sensuous creature
has no room left
to see all the colour
above its head,
its fluttery future,
much less
acknowledge kinship.

Fractured glass,
these jewels stringing my days
are already broken

the light
shows all these fissures

fragile,
misshapen
only if I am blinded
by some ideal

otherwise
shaped as they are,

splintered and shining.

A polished paddle,
well designed
for keeping me on course

crafted for hope and confidence

it is good
to practice these strokes,
thrust
and gentle curves
to pull backwards,

avoid needless crashes.

The river is fiercely benign;
losing my paddle
can feel like torment

— sometimes I am asked
to lay it by my feet,
explore life
with no compass —

sometimes it is flung
out of my canoe,
wrenched from my grasp
by the force of water.

Empty-handed,
I would practice trust
as a last resort,
a radical curiosity,

but today
my fingers cling
to the sides of the boat,

terror has me frozen

until I somehow hear the joke,
understand that clutching
will not save me

allow my face
to be twitched
in a grimace like a grin

understand that capsizing
is inevitable

loosen just a little,
intrigued.

The shape of my heart
is changing
I feel my ribs
cracking

the way pleasure and pain
arrive entwined

the dough of love
is rising
like a breadpan overfull

messy and ecstatic

here in the glow
of my chest

I hear my hands and feet
protest like distant cousins,
feel my midriff
try to belt itself again

know the shape
of who I was
has left me

my hands
reaching for questions

the fire only laughs.

16

Some seeds
do take longer
to sprout
and reach for sky

this is not an apology;
a fact of garden

subterranean truth.

We who have a habit
of letting our eyes lead
see barren ground

the belly of the earth
carries communities,
microbes and minerals
succouring seeds
that have split open wide
unseen
dropping downwards
and upwards
in the warm resistance
that carries their tendrils.

Close your eyes
if they only show you
an empty field,
promise and loss;
what is happening
underground
is real.

10 Virgins

Fidelity to dreams
— I don't mean hopes

but mossy uprisings
in the night,
keeping one hand
on spongy dark wet
even in daylight

letting my lamp
be filled with oil daily,
ready for darkness
and joy's unexpected arrival,
ready to light up
in greeting.

The five with this practice
sound severe
refusing their lazy sisters,
but actually they can't share;
each oil unique,
filtered through rock and moss,
collected reverently.

O may I hear all ten,
listen to them jostle inside,
encourage five to stay alert
and five to seek oil
for their chapped hearts.

Matthew 25:1-13

My sister grouse
with your tiny brain
and big butt
running in panic

forgetting you have wings
in the forward motion
of your anxiety

letting adrenalin
ruin your capacity
to remember who you are...

how beautifully
your fucked up response
reminds me tenderly
of me.

I carry
an old story
of unrequited love

like all tales
there is truth in it

how nothing is ever enough

how no thing is enough

there is enough in no thing

and everything.

Love will burn
as fully as I let it in;
the skies
will not let me touch them

and yet I can burn
when they touch me

let magenta and gold
live here.

I noticed my waking
like after a chinook

cold had been intense
requiring persistence

and warm wind
had blown its tender chaos
while I was mostly sleeping

and I woke
to this mild world
wind abated
silence spreading.

I want to make room
for the wild wind

can feel it whispering
around my open windows

the door is ajar
and mostly stillness
enters in

receptive longing
channelled these grooves,
washed space
through all this mud

the dancing howl
I'm waiting for
may never arrive

and I can sit
to feel soft breeze
on naked skin.

Night Waking

We met
in almost darkness
my car open
to his apology

she had asked me
to find the door

and since words failed
I came to demonstrate

but they had found their own entry
by the time I roused from bed.

The joy in this late night scribbling
comes from honesty

how I am just recording
what happened

even as metaphor
drips, midnight rain.

Frail

a word spoken in judgement
to divide,
beat down in lack,
accentuate risk

or spoken in kindness
to hold,
nurture as precious,
accentuate risk

we all stretch gossamer lives
across our holes,
oscillating

different tones of frailty

sounding.

Perhaps you missed
hearing yourself in the story

how a guy
was just barely keeping afloat
and a helper
jumped out of the boat
and started to cling

with uncontrolled
natural
human impulses

imperilling them both.

How instead
there are ways to call
encouragement

to offer things that float
and temporary cords

to let the ocean
do its carrying work

to know that exertion
and tears of love
and waves themselves
are salty.

Give thanks
for gifts arising

even when they look
like trouble

even when you know
that horse is full of soldiers

even when they come
to take away your blankets;

remember your beloved
hides in plain view

rise from your comforts
for the welcoming.

I choose to proclaim
my bond with you

through right of kinship;

we share the same DNA

even as with fish
and beetles.

I thought I needed you
to notice me
and had a sense of waiting

but now my bells
ring in silent time

happy pealing
resonant
unnoticed
except in my fibres,
these tendrils intertwined.

A juicy goddess
with an armload of
sweet produce

taps her foot
not so patiently

while the bureaucrat
taking up space in my heart
fills out forms;

assesses risk and liability,
trying to compute predictions

enjoying the small-minded
power of control

the red pen,
triplicate copies.

Woe is me
if she turns on her heel;
this desk between us
must be shoved aside.

Such vital surgery

to separate love
from the objects of our affections;

the way I can see aurora and comets
where you see a normal night sky

or strive to sleep under it.

The flashing of love
is visible and real

and never entirely shared

and sometimes not at all;

the wound of love

is only belief that it should be.

Give me a surgeon's hand
to gently slice my illusions,
receive the gifts of living
without needing them attached;

love coursing through a million stars
as I stand alone
and part of it.

The vertigo of being alive

this nausea on the edge
when I pause the spinning
to listen to air

no fix
and nothing to moan about

a wobble
signalling life

so many fancy stories
to camouflage

this is not pain
or pleasure

and I thought equanimity
would be
more comfortable.

My greed
is like this:
wanting to use
all the colours
at once,
so joyous their possibility

and yet I know
that mixing all the shades
makes mud

and while earth tones
are real and lovely

I can also learn
to make these tiny spots
of variation,
passionate hues
in pixellation

and the shapes
will show themselves
regardless.

These rituals of season,
bikes to be stored
in advance of snow

harvesting after frost

me falling in love again
with unreachable clouds

needing new lingerie
to add to the laundry pile

… with gratitude today,
reverence not despair

I see how this season
is not the same
as the last dance

familiar themes
but differently deeper

spiralling closer to flame.

Life is
painfully beautiful

and it makes me mad
that only a slight shift
in emphasis

is what we get to choose;

painfully beautiful,

life itself refuses

to offer emphasis,

is unmoving
in weighting both;

knows that our choice
is meaningless,
offering nothing
with open hands

beautifully painful.

It really is
all about God

although it sounds trite
to the mind alone

the body vibrates
when it hears
the truth

how God flows out
and comes to visit
in tender disguise
as enemy and lover
and often both.

I've been a little short
on noticing;
awe spilled in today
like precious oil
expanding a cramped heart;
a plucked string
calming all vibration
in one sure note;
kindness receiving its own hands
in welcome.

Help me to seek safety
in the flow of kindness,
drop the endless want,
sink into the pond
where we settle
with hearts visible and beating.

Let this fatigue
be a cushion
from which love can flow
without effort

forcing me to rest
my intentions,
heart spreadeagled
and helpless

a generous surrender

a skilful noticing
I have nothing left to offer

empty cup,
a puddle on the floor.

The diagnosis
might actually come
later today

you are in cold dread
and I have been laughing
as if it isn't true

both of us so foolish.

The diagnosis
is written on our foreheads,
these wrinkled brows
that crave a tender touch

on soft fontanelles,
on newly rugged shoulders

dependent leaves of houseplants.

Just this:
wake up from denial,
rise from fear's cold trance

lubricate the heart,
enjoy warmth while it lasts

care deeply.

My Siamese twin
distorts this chest,
twists this true alignment
by the fact
we share one heart

she drones
dissatisfied lament
with all the breath
I give her

we share
belly and legs,
freedom of choice
constricted

even as I journey
accompanied

by her grasping.

Wise ones
have shaken heads;
surgery doomed,
I cannot feed her overmuch
without peril.

Oh, let me welcome
the gift
of four hands,
sixteen fingers and four thumbs
to caress the world.

So much of how we live
is non-verbal

vibrations between stars
hold our planet

tingling and cold
in our limbs
point to stories
we have no words for

shadow and light
the moving pigment
of our days.

Hula dancers,
shift this knowing
into gesture,
let its waving
shape us

moved by what is here.

My great-grandmother
was flighty

or so the story goes

and seemed to spend
unwonted time
with hats and dresses

my grandmother serious,
curious,
a radical hiding in white gloves

my mother
felt subversive
from birth,
decades of rebellion
in mild costumes,
longing for sky

my butterfly lineage.

These epic tasks
are laughably small
and still feel insurmountable

like a chick
in terror, pushing
and hungry

I know I must eat my shell

taste chalky discomfort

consume my limitations
even as I mourn
how they have held me safe;

find freedom
and squat naked
where the breeze is.

Equanimity like a soft moan;
I had thought it was a high plateau
for safe viewing,
open space for opposites
to roll in new possibility,
freedom vista

and while this can be true,
there is a valley too,
a raw gap
where desire
trails hot fingers
on a cold chest,
where fear and longing for light
almost collide,
the equanimity of gasp,
small pocket of air
breathless
empty
awe.

My kite
is tugging fiercely
from its height

I want to run,
follow its lead

fear adrenalin
will blind me
to where I will stumble

notice
that chasing kites
means trusting wind
or strings will shorten

feel the tension
of indecision

forward, backward
standing still.

Kite, string,
me with uncertain grip

only wind
is real

the rest of it
following

held and blown,
hurtling
wafting

different directions
for falling.

The path of my kite
may lead
through dens of inequity,
past brigands
and biting beasts

running with abandon
and plentiful resistance

kite soaring
feet pushing ground

windsong.

May angels dance
on my tongue today

freeing up my voice
for good silence

relaxing my jaw
to speak truth
without armour.

In fact,
let them dance there all day
with no room
for me to get the words out

if there is no need

the angels know
when to stop
fluttering wings

to make room
for sweet wind

I can just hold space
for their cavorting.

Fear
used to live in me
like a toddler

unruly
and loud

pulling my belly
like it was hair

no boundaries,
confident
I'd never let it go.

Over the years
it learned to relax,
my love more firm
about where it could live.

Nowadays fear
is like a young man
in the rigging,
swaying a little in wind,
alerting me to rocks,
feeding at my table,
not my breast.

Someday fear may move on,
sending letters home,
acknowledging our deep connection.

Jumping monkeys squabbling,
let me concede defeat

stop trying to calm them

let go of impossible shape
I imagine as peace

let the shaking begin

jump freely
in no direction

listen to my babble
without judgement

bounce on the bed;

agitation too is real.

Last week
there was a lama
in my basement

— this sounds like dream
or metaphor
but was real —

I crept each day
to make space
and offer blessings.

And learned
that any traveller
is beloved.

And relish now
the pleasure
of shaking dust
each day
from my lush red carpet,

new arrivals.

I walk
one foot and then another,
sometimes looking for adventure
and thinking it is elsewhere

and yet when I move each foot
tenderly
or stoop
to pick up socks
or wipe a messy counter
yet again

and listen
for invitations

I feel the sonar
touch my heart,
words like far-off calling
travelling to my receiver,

feel the sustaining precision
of being where I need to be
to hear my companions
distant and near,

move in these rituals
that look so ordinary.

Problem-solving

Chess pieces,
I used strategic thought

anticipating moves,
imagining new positions

trying to control the action

wanting to strengthen
wisdom muscles.

Nowadays
my attention lingers
on carved faces,
how we pivot and dart;
looking for more detail,
curiosity and love
prompt my urge to see.

O let these glances
of clarity
nudge my trail,
let me move on black and white
propelled by unseen hands,
drop my pursuit of conquest,
welcome all patterns of being,
smile at faces coming into range.

How beautiful,
that burden
you are dragging
up a hill

not the first climb

all that clanking
of rusty armour
making you strong
and crippled

sweat, blood,
calloused hands,
fortitude;

here at the crest
of the piercing view

will your fingers release?

Like a toddler's grip
on illusion of "mine,"
can each little finger
be coaxed

to open and let fall?

Dance
untethered?

Of course
I am greedy for joy

of course
I want the people
to dance in their pain
the way I have learned
that we can

of course
my natural instinct
is to cling
to dreams of happiness
tinged with tears of beauty

and visions of kindness
healing us all
in creative touch
we can barely imagine

and fields of oats
nodding their heads in kinship

endless waves of invitation.

I am water;
a glass is being tipped
and I fall
soundless
until another glass
angles to meet my descent

in the air
light glints
on the process of my spilling.

The sound of my landing
keeps changing
as the new glass
also tips,
propelling me forward,
yet more space
in which to drop
unheard.

Like a water wheel,
but this organic shape
defies my need to know;
the shining as I fall
refracts for others,
may cause more tipping elsewhere;

we are a net of water
falling endlessly.

Conversation in a snowstorm

I can't tell
which voices belong
to what is thrown

ice shards
come whistling past my ears,
white feathers
falling in return

normally soul
is softer,
ego brittle

but perhaps this storm
is trying to teach me
something cold

feathers, snowflakes, crystals
all here.

I have a handful
of small treasures,
rubies and sapphires,
emerald moments

and yearnings for more

they are so beautiful,
rare,
filled with rainbows.

And this is a curious dance,
to let them fall,
expose them for the taking,
give up the hoarding
and plotting to gain

let the umbilicus of time
feed me what I need

gasp in awe
as the treasures
swirl away.

My heart goes out

to people who fall

when they didn't expect to;

feel themselves listening
for a knock at the door

feel breath catch
in greeting

a bellyful of anticipation
fed by an empty throat.

Lovers engaged with a world

more intense

than yesterday's,

vibrating with promise

and nothing promised,

sweet anguish.

These epic journeys
one foot lifted,
one landing,
one lifting...

or wind on wingtips
now
and rising slightly
and veering left,
descending just a little
or flapping
as up
and down
and upstroke yet again

until a thousand miles
has been traversed

or maybe
just to the corner

and equally epic.

This tale of almost,

two vials with potential

for chemical reaction,

a heart smoldering

but not quite ignited,

a love unrequited

over and over,

a sheaf of papers

not quite a novel,

a distance vision

except for cloudy veil,

two feet almost touching ground,

willingness

to land and fly.

I had some stories
of poison
and how I wanted
to stop drinking it

how I could clean
the contours of my soul
with bright light

now I see how I can change

can choose to drink
the strong elixir

be more courageous
in greeting what is here;

deep welcome
to vitality

astringent
pungent

real.

The computer
and stories of lists
had sapped me again

and I hobbled outside

to find sun
on frost-killed pansies.

In sisterhood
with their shrivelled loveliness
I let sun and breath
warm my wrinkles
visible and invisible

...noticed buds
and spent attentive time
with scissors
and a jug of water

...not a waste of time,
even though death is coming soon.

My tender heart,
tending,
is how I pulse.

I can be more brave.

I have been a coward in love,

afraid to let it spill on the curb

afraid to laugh with abandon

at the parking guy,

share my paltry secrets

with crow or cashier.

I have feared bubbling

with strangers

and with my intimate friends,

fear of scalding

fear of foolish falls.

Today I relinquish my limbs

to the Jester;

let joy and wit

tremble awkwardly,

spark what they will.

An architect
with intricate and large designs,
these papers
must be laid down
on the earth

be touched
and turn soggy,
a compost gift.

A gardener
has need of this soil,
willing to wait
for the season of planting,
watching for the ways
that sprouting will happen,
the long pull
of harvest
after unforeseen tomorrows.

Even in autumn,
this wet ground,
stark patch of possibility
unhurried,
smelling faintly of yesterday,
a necessary dormancy
even as fistfuls of microbes
keep moving.

I'm so attached
to beauty,
the way that water
melts rivulets
in my iceberg,
water like sculptor
shaping these patterns

intricate coldness,
gorgeous spikes of crystal
shards of frozen anemone

this pathos
burning yet more melting,
highlighting regret
of change,
how I loathe
the loss of form
even as I welcome flow

how my tears
can land as glass
or lost in ocean.

Surrender has a sadness

but water and ice
have no difference,
sameness changing shape.

My ego is like a gong
summoning throughout the day

I now live
in this quieter retreat

but the gong clangs
often
with its demands

and I am getting better
at rising from my tasks
with less urgency,
wrapping my robes
so I can walk,
storing my tools
so as not to create clutter.

Together we sit
again
the clang reverberating,
listening to echoes of need,
residues of injustice,
promptings of fear and anger

letting them oscillate
because they do

paying attention.

If God lives here
then we're all in trouble

this messed-up bunch of holes
is just a shell
through which light pours

I am not God
even as I hear
God say I Am

happy, messed-up
mystery.

His name was Yu
the sound of my name
sometimes

and when he pointed out
an intimate unpleasantness
I did not run

but gathered necessary strength

and the battle was simple,
won with no violence.

And you
who feels vanquished
from time to time

temporarily

remember that help
is sometimes obvious.

This week I heard a story
of distorted love

an odd shape to caring and craving
late in life

like a hairdresser and old lady
… no matter the costumes.

What I see
is how I long for happy endings,
wish I could pour healing
on the one who craves
so she can cling a little less,
give voice to the one who cares
and neglects the call of courage

an elixir
for the sweet tilt,

shifting love from ugly

finding brightness.

I am peeling
like an orange
on offer,
sweet and bitter both

trying to be still
for moments,
consummate savouring
until there is no centre, essential space

and in that cherished empty

gratitude for rind

for a peel
cut in service

offering something solid
for others to hold more easily
as they eat

odd generosity,
a thicker skin.

When I say God

I mean the one that isn't;

formless

nameless

empty.

And so I have no name

for spacious love,

for kindness that links,

for the weaving

of unseen patterns;

too many names

crowding my tongue

which is why

I sometimes stop

wagging it.

The grass is plenty green
right here

even though there is snow on it
and I'm old enough
to remember the despair
of dry brown in spring

even so,
it's green enough.

Oh, I've checked out
my neighbours' gardens
and been envious

have seen what looks lush
and wanted to go there

as if rolling on another lawn
were more fun

but the clouds look the same
lying on this one

and it's plenty green
sometimes.

I've spent too long
outside the lap of god

as if trudging alone
is more fair
to those who cry

now I find the spring
in my step
to leap

to notice my need
for fuzzy blankets

to feel how this joyful perch
allows me to see
while I snuggle.

Stomping through the woods,
fuzzy-headed with craving,
frantic with not-having

and equally disdaining,
turning from all
that provokes my no

this ambivalent heart
could run an engine
back and forth

tragic waste of time

until the lens becomes
sufficiently third person

with a mona lisa smile.

I sit
on this incline
a mountain at my back

watching the view,
a man with a shovel
and a fever for gold

and while my climb
will call me
to thinner air

let my heart ignite
in the heat of digging,
give me the passionate sweat
of longing for what is here,
a pointed spade
uncovering this treasure,
removing all that keeps it hidden

these veins of bright
exposed and on offer

exertion in service
to mountain.

Really
there are just three poems:

oww

aah

and the silent one between them.

It's all about God.

I would hold your hand
and walk you to safety

but right now
I'm ignited
like a burning bush

and have no clue

what will injure you
or heal

have burned
the karmic map I used to know

this fire
so far beyond
right and wrong.

I hope some warmth
touches your chill

this blaze too
is me.

Somehow the story
of bushel baskets
hiding light

got twisted

I heard it as salvation
the safe alternative
to burning in the night

the modesty of hiding

of wanting god
to come find me.

This hide and seek

is done

a child's game

I have outgrown,

sparks heated

by the world around me,

a flicker
of charred wicker.

Matthew 5:15

Save me
from being too pious

give me reverence
like a big wind
that could crush me
but chooses not to

blowing through
and all around

a sweet violence.

Help me to relax
in my ignorance

so my heart
has room for knowing.

Help me to hunker down
without bunkering

stripped naked
with desire
for what is here.

This Beloved
I call for
is trying to reach our her hands,
lifting his eyes to catch mine,
calling in different voices,
keeping me awake,
enticing me to sleep.

The names
are now getting silly,
tales of loneliness and welcome,
tingling and tasty,
terrible and tragic,
swirling in caves
that are mine
and never were.

it is not enough
to know that I might crack up,
eggshell of body and heart and mind
too fragile
for this gale of love;

even this truth
can't stop me
from begging for more.

Tapas

Subversive

this loitering,

only because it is so rare,

the lack of agenda

sitting in public

a genuine hello

no protection

being in love

without owning,

wallowing

in warm soup

while others follow hunger,

each taste rich.

O love
with too many names

I want to slurp you
like a slushie

feel the loud sucking
of lack
when I have drained the cup

and laugh
with its refilling, endlessly.

I want to be slurped
as an offering

saying no to nothing,

giving again and again

in reckless joy,

life dancing

because it can.

All of these scratchings
are love poems

how even the soft primrose
is covered in thorns
and leaves its rich fruit
like a late joke
in winter

shrivelled and sweet

how I let a maudlin longing
for delicate pink
and early summer

prevent me from tasting
this prickly kindness.